THE STRANGER

CHRIS VAN ALLSBURG

Houghton Mifflin Company

Boston 1986

To my mother and father

Library of Congress Cataloging-in-Publication Data

Van Allsburg, Chris.
  The stranger.

  Summary: The enigmatic origins of the stranger
Farmer Bailey hits with his truck and brings home
to recuperate seem to have a mysterious relation
to the weather.
  I. Title.
PZ7.V266St   1986   [Fic]   86-15235
ISBN 0-395-42331-7

Printed in the United States of America

10 9 8 7 6 5 4 3 2 1
N S

THE STRANGER

It was the time of year Farmer Bailey liked best, when summer turned to fall. He whistled as he drove along. A cool breeze blew across his face through the truck's open window. Then it happened. There was a loud "thump." Mr. Bailey jammed on his brakes. "Oh no!" he thought. "I've hit a deer."

But it wasn't a deer the farmer found lying in the road, it was a man. Mr. Bailey knelt down beside the still figure, fearing the worst. Then, suddenly, the man opened his eyes. He looked up with terror and jumped to his feet. He tried to run off, lost his balance, and fell down. He got up again, but this time the farmer took his arm and helped him to the truck.

Mr. Bailey drove home. He helped the stranger inside, where Mrs. Bailey made him comfortable on the parlor sofa. Katy, their daughter, peeked into the room. The man on the sofa was dressed in odd rough leather clothing. She heard her father whisper "...must be some kind of hermit...sort of fellow who lives alone in the woods." The stranger didn't seem to understand the questions Mr. Bailey asked him. "I don't think," whispered Mrs. Bailey, "he knows how to talk."

Mr. Bailey called the doctor, who came and listened to the stranger's heart, felt his bones, looked in his eyes, and took his temperature. He decided the man had lost his memory. There was a bump on the back of his head. "In a few days," the doctor said, "he should remember who he is and where he's from." Mrs. Bailey stopped the doctor as he left the house. He'd forgotten his thermometer. "Oh, you can throw that out," he answered. "It's broken, the mercury is stuck at the bottom."

Mr. Bailey lent the stranger some clean clothes. The fellow seemed confused about buttonholes and buttons. In the evening he joined the Baileys for dinner. The steam that rose from the hot food fascinated him. He watched Katy take a spoonful of soup and blow gently across it. Then he did exactly the same. Mrs. Bailey shivered. "Brrr," she said. "There's a draft in here tonight."

The next morning Katy watched the stranger from her bedroom window. He walked across the yard, toward two rabbits. Instead of running into the woods, the rabbits took a hop in his direction. He picked one of them up and stroked its ears, then set it down. The rabbits hopped away, then stopped and looked back, as if they expected the stranger to follow.

When Katy's father went into the fields that day, the stranger shyly tagged along. Mr. Bailey gave him a pitchfork and, with a little practice, he learned to use it well. They worked hard. Occasionally Mr. Bailey would have to stop and rest. But the stranger never tired. He didn't even sweat.

That evening Katy sat with the stranger, watching the setting sun. High above them a flock of geese, in perfect V formation, flew south on the trip that they made every fall. The stranger could not take his eyes off the birds. He stared at them like a man who'd been hypnotized.

Two weeks passed and the stranger still could not remember who he was. But the Baileys didn't mind. They liked having the stranger around. He had become one of the family. Day by day he'd grown less timid. "He seems so happy to be around us," Mr. Bailey said to his wife. "It's hard to believe he's a hermit."

Another week passed. Farmer Bailey could not help noticing how peculiar the weather had been. Not long ago it seemed that autumn was just around the corner. But now it still felt like summer, as if the seasons couldn't change. The warm days made the pumpkins grow larger than ever. The leaves on the trees were as green as they'd been three weeks before.

One day the stranger climbed the highest hill on the Bailey farm. He looked to the north and saw a puzzling sight. The trees in the distance were bright red and orange. But the trees to the south, like those round the Baileys', were nothing but shades of green. They seemed so drab and ugly to the stranger. It would be much better, he thought, if all trees could be red and orange.

The stranger's feelings grew stronger the next day. He couldn't look at a tree's green leaves without sensing that something was terribly wrong. The more he thought about it, the more upset he became, until finally he could think of nothing else. He ran to a tree and pulled off a leaf. He held it in a trembling hand and, without thinking, blew on it with all his might.

At dinner that evening the stranger appeared dressed in his old leather clothes. By the tears in his eyes the Baileys could tell that their friend had decided to leave. He hugged them all once, then dashed out the door. The Baileys hurried outside to wave good-bye, but the stranger had disappeared. The air had turned cold, and the leaves on the trees were no longer green.

Every autumn since the stranger's visit, the same thing happens at the Bailey farm. The trees that surround it stay green for a week after the trees to the north have turned. Then overnight they change their color to the brightest of any tree around. And etched in frost on the farmhouse windows are words that say simply, "See you next fall."

The type is set in Garamond #3 by Litho Composition Company, Inc.
The paper is Lustro Offset Enamel Dull, supplied by S.D. Warren Company.
Both text and jacket are printed by Case–Hoyt Corporation.
The books are bound by Nicholstone Book Bindery.